LISTENER'S GUIDE

In CLASSICAL *mood*

Shades of Autumn

Shades of Autumn

The season of autumn, bidding farewell to the happy days of summer in one last glorious display of color, is one of the most poignant of nature's moods. It is not surprising then, that the sweet melancholy of those autumnal days has inspired some of the world's most touching music. In this volume of *In Classical Mood* you will find some of the great composers' responses to this most invigorating season. Vivaldi's magnificent *Four Seasons*, Tchaikovsky's gently moving *Chant sans paroles*, and Mozart's reflective *Piano Concerto No.23* will all transport you into a world of beauty.

THE LISTENER'S GUIDE – WHAT THE SYMBOLS MEAN

THE COMPOSERS
Their lives... their loves..
their legacies...

THE MUSIC
Explanation... analysis...
interpretation...

THE INSPIRATION
How works of genius
came to be written

THE BACKGROUND
People, places, and events
linked to the music

© MCMXCVII IMP AB   In Classical Mood™   IMP AB, produced under license by IMP Inc.   Printed in China.   US P 2201 12 013

Contents

– 2 –
The Four Seasons: Autumn
ANTONIO VIVALDI

– 4 –
Chant sans paroles No.3, Opus 2
PYOTR TCHAIKOVSKY

– 5 –
Autumn
CÉCILE CHAMINADE

– 8 –
The Victorian Kitchen Garden Suite: Mists
PAUL READE

– 9 –
Lyric Pieces No.1, Opus 12: Arietta
EDVARD GRIEG

– 10 –
Piano Concerto No.23 in A K488: Second Movement
WOLFGANG AMADEUS MOZART

– 12 –
Evening Rhapsody
JOACHIM RAFF

– 15 –
Cello Concerto: First Movement (Excerpt)
SIR EDWARD ELGAR

– 16 –
A London Symphony: Second Movement
RALPH VAUGHAN WILLIAMS

– 18 –
Images (For Orchestra): Gigues
CLAUDE DEBUSSY

– 20 –
Lieutenant Kijé: Romance
SERGEI PROKOFIEV

– 23 –
The Seasons: Autumn ("Bacchanale" and "Petit Adagio")
ALEXANDER GLAZUNOV

THE FOUR SEASONS: AUTUMN

ANTONIO VIVALDI 1678–1741

The Four Seasons

AUTUMN

The vibrant rhythm of Vivaldi's opening movement transports the listener into a rustic scene of peasants dancing on a warm autumn evening. When the solo violin enters, it does so decisively, adding vigor to the dance with its runs up and down the scale and double-stopping (where two strings are held down and played together). The contrast of slower, more reflective moments anticipates the night's approach. A hypnotic section brings us to the day's end, with the peasants gradually falling into a contented slumber, but stirred by a brief return to the initial jollity, which concludes the movement.

MUSICAL POETRY

A *sonnetto dimostrativo* (illustrative sonnet) accompanies each movement. For "Autumn," it is: "The peasant celebrates with song and dance, His joys in the fulsome harvest, And with the cup of Bacchus so o'erwhelmed, His revels in sleep are drowned."

THE FOUR SEASONS: AUTUMN

THE AMSTERDAM CONNECTION

In 1737, Vivaldi had been commissioned to stage three operas in Ferrara, northern Italy, over a three-year period. Though he rarely left his home in Venice, Vivaldi decided to travel to Amsterdam *(right)* the following year. There in Holland his work had been published for many years and he was even more popular than in his native Italy. Unfortunately, Vivaldi met with some conflict upon his return. His wrangling and stubbornness over his fee for the commissioned operas angered the theater patrons so much that the Cardinal of Ferrara refused him entry into the city.

MIXED REACTIONS

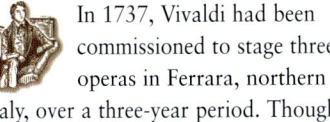

The celebrated virtuoso violinist Nigel Kennedy *(left)* brought *The Four Seasons* to a much wider public in his 1985 recording, making it one of the biggest-selling pieces of classical music ever. His interpretation of the music was acclaimed for its exuberance and vitality, although some critics were unhappy with his use of the wooden part of the bow to add percussion during some sequences.

KEY NOTES

Vivaldi was famous for writing music at a remarkable speed. When his friend De Brosses had first met the composer in the autumn of 1739, he remarked that he had observed Vivaldi "compose a concerto with all its different parts more quickly than a copyist could note it down."

Chant sans paroles No. 3, Opus 2

Pyotr Tchaikovsky
1840–1893

Chant sans paroles
No. 3, Opus 2

This elegant and gently romantic composition for piano evokes a sense of autumnal tranquility and is in marked contrast to some of Pyotr Tchaikovsky's more passionate compositions. The piece starts reflectively in waltz time followed by a faster dramatic section. The opening melody briefly returns and is taken up by the piano before dying away.

Serene and Charming

Tchaikovsky composed more than a hundred small piano works, most of which he called "pieces." They reflect a more serene side to his nature. It is hard to imagine how the composer of such passionate and heartrending orchestral music could also produce such peaceful and charming short piano works.

Key Notes

Tchaikovsky was often blunt regarding other composers, except for the few he admired such as Mozart. He described Handel as "fourth-rate," confessed he could not tolerate Brahms, and thought Wagner had "killed his colossal genius with theories."

Autumn

CÉCILE CHAMINADE *1857–1944*

Autumn

In this powerfully emotive piece by one of the world's few renowned female composers, the violin's full range is utilized to give breadth to the passionate melody. The music takes the violin from its lowest to its highest notes with the autumnal refrain echoed by the lower strings of the orchestra. A more fervent mood emerges, which increases in tension until the original melody returns, this time mingling passion with a hint of regret. At the conclusion, the violin soars to the top of its range before the music gently fades away.

Destined for a Brilliant Career

Cécile Chaminade *(below left)* was only eight years old when Bizet declared that she was "destined for a brilliant career." He soon started performing her own compositions in her native Paris, and her exceptional piano skills won acclaim from both critics and public alike. She started to make regular tours abroad, residing permanently in her home in Monte Carlo *(right)*. Though a gifted and versatile composer, Chaminade is perhaps best remembered for her short piano pieces, which, if lacking in depth, still have a charm that is elegantly conveyed—it is salon music at its best.

Diverse Influences

Chaminade wrote several works in various styles and forms, including orchestral music, ballets, comic opera, and songs, as well as more than two hundred piano works. Her versatility as a composer owed a great deal to those she studied under, namely Le Couppey, Savart, Marsick, and Godard *(right)*. Two of these composers are worth a special mention: Marsick for his evocative orchestration in his operas, such as *Lara*, and Godard, whose chamber music, symphonies, concertos, and songs made him immensely popular during his own lifetime. Sadly, Godard's works have been largely forgotten, and he is now only really remembered for *Berceuse* from his opera *Jocelyn*.

AUTUMN

OTHER WOMEN COMPOSERS

Possibly the first woman to make her mark in music was the 12th-century German mystic Hildegard of Bingen *(right)*. She wrote many poems, which she set to music, as well as many religious compositions. Women composers of the 19th century included Fanny Mendelssohn (1805–1847), sister of Felix and a gifted songwriter, and Clara Schumann (1819–1896), wife of Robert, who wrote many beautiful compositions. The English composer Ethel Smyth (1858–1944) holds a unique place in musical history. An advocate of the women's movement of the early 1900s, Smyth *(left)* was imprisoned in 1911. In jail, she composed *March of the Women* and used a toothbrush for a baton to conduct it.

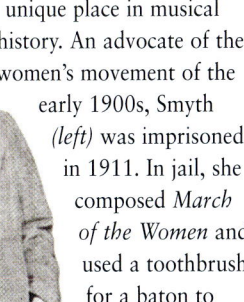

THE BOULANGER SISTERS

Two other French women who scaled the heights in the world of music were the Boulanger sisters, Nadia (1887–1979) and Lili (1893–1918). Nadia *(below, top)* was noted worldwide as a teacher of composition whose pupils included Aaron Copland. She was also a leading conductor and was the first woman to conduct a complete concert of the Royal Philharmonic Society in London. Her younger sister Lili, was a highly gifted composer. Despite her ill health, Lili *(right)* became the first woman to win the Prix de Rome, five years before her death at just twenty-five years old.

KEY NOTES

Originally a charming salon piece for piano from Six études de concert *("Six Concert Studies"), Chaminade's* Autumn *was later orchestrated by Paul Uy for the violinist Michael Guttman. It is this arrangement for violin and orchestra that is included here.*

The Victorian Kitchen Garden Suite: Mists

Paul Reade *1943–1997*

Victorian Kitchen Garden Suite

Mists

There could hardly be a more beautiful combination than that of the velvety sound of the clarinet and the ethereal yet crystal-clear sound of the harp. The blend that results brings to mind the varied colors found in the kitchen garden of a typical 19th-century country house. The colors can also be compared to the brilliant shades of autumn's changing leaves. Reade insisted the piece "be played with a lingering autumnal feeling" and it certainly evokes a sense of nostalgia for an era now past.

Composing for Television

The English composer Paul Reade was born in London. He had many successes in television music, including the theme for *Jane Eyre*. He also wrote a number of fine works for concert performance, including two aesthetic pieces: *Prelude* for piano and clarinet, and *Romanze*, a waltz for strings and a saxophone quartet.

Key Notes

Reade's Suite, consisting of five pieces entitled Prelude, Spring, Mists, Exotica, *and* Summer *included the signature tune for the popular British TV series* The Victorian Kitchen Garden.

LYRIC PIECES, NO. 1, OPUS 12 : ARIETTA

EDVARD GRIEG *1843–1907*

Lyric Pieces

NO. 1, OPUS 12: ARIETTA

The melody of this short piece for piano is direct and simple, while its use of repeated notes is wistful and romantic. Addressed to a mysterious girl, it has a sad, reflective feel throughout—perhaps recalling the experiences and memories of love on a quiet autumn's evening. Grieg wrote this piece with the amateur pianist in mind, to be performed for an intimate gathering of family or friends. As a result, its range of expression is relatively restrained, although this in no way detracts from its charm.

GRIEG'S SCOTTISH HERITAGE

Grieg's great-grandfather, Alexander Greig, was born in Scotland. He left his native country during the Battle of Culloden in 1746, though his leaving had more to do with the economic hardships in the Highlands rather than political reasons. He settled in Norway where the spelling of Greig was changed to Grieg.

KEY NOTES

It was probably Edvard Grieg who first coined the term lyric piece *to describe a small piano work that concentrated on mood rather than form. Arietta opens the first of five volumes of such piano works, the last volume being later orchestrated as the* Lyric Suite.

PIANO CONCERTO NO. 23 IN A K488: SECOND MOVEMENT

WOLFGANG AMADEUS MOZART 1756–1791

Piano Concerto No. 23 in A

K488: SECOND MOVEMENT

A deep sense of emotion runs through the piano's hesitant opening, which contrasts with the brooding of the strings and haunting woodwind refrains that follow. The piano gently soothes the feelings of despair called up by the orchestra. A short interlude follows in which the clarinet, joined briefly by the piano, strikes a more optimistic mood. But, like shadows lengthening at the end of an autumn day, the more reflective mood returns. Toward the end, an air of serenity is introduced with a sparse piano melody accompanied by pizzicato strings.

LIMITED RANGE

Pianos in Mozart's time were limited to five octaves. Some had two knee levers for sustaining the bass or treble tone separately—a feature Mozart exploited.

PIANO CONCERTO NO.23 IN A K488: SECOND MOVEMENT

MOZART'S YEARS OF DECLINE

The year 1786, when the *Piano Concerto No.23*, the *Prague Symphony*, and *The Marriage of Figaro* were all composed, was a turning point in Mozart's life. Musically he was at the height of his powers, but his creative genius was not rewarded with financial success. Despite the triumph of *Figaro*, he was unable to gain a secure post at the Viennese court. His financial situation went from bad to

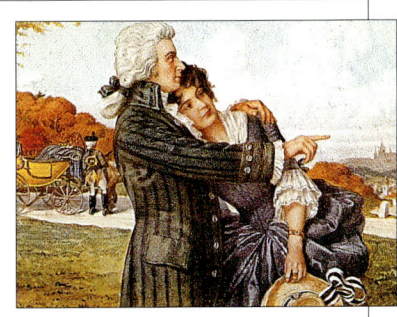

worse, not helped by the illness of his wife Constanze *(above)* to whom he was devoted. Mozart's begging letters to the Viennese merchant Michael Puchberg pitifully reveal his despair. But in the end, his own failing health—the inevitable result of constant strain, anxiety, and poor eating—sped him to an early death *(left)* and a final, tragic resting place in an unmarked public grave.

MOZART AND SALIERI

The truth behind Mozart and Salieri's relationship, which later inspired the play and film *Amadeus*, is unknown. It is thought that Mozart, near his death, believed that Salieri was trying to poison him. But this was probably due to Mozart's weak mental state rather than facts themselves. Supposedly, Salieri was one of a mere handful to attend Mozart's funeral.

KEY NOTES

In the Piano Concerto No.23 in A Major and in the Piano Concerto No.22 in E-flat, Mozart chose not to write any parts for the oboe. He used clarinets instead of oboes in the woodwind section to add a smooth velvety texture to the music.

EVENING RHAPSODY

JOACHIM RAFF *1822–1882*

Evening Rhapsody

A sumptuous wash of strings conjures up the spectacular mountainous countryside of Raff's native Switzerland. The melody brings in the horn and then the oboe, and as each instrument comes in, Raff's deep passion for the landscape is revealed. The piece shows a strong influence of Wagner, with deliberate echoes of the yearning love duet from his opera *Tristan and Isolde* in the tortuous rising phrases and tension-filled harmonies. Orchestral swells and rolling kettledrums add to the overall grandeur as the music rises to a passionate climax before the Alpine autumn evening draws to a close.

Self-taught Musician

Though Joachim Raff is recognized as a Swiss composer, his family was German in origin. He was born in the village of Lachen near Lake Zurich *(below)* after his father had fled to Switzerland to avoid being enlisted as a soldier. Raff was largely self-taught, but his skill attracted the backing of two great talents. First, Felix Mendelssohn arranged for Raff's early piano pieces to be printed. Then, in 1845, Raff walked to Basle to meet Franz Liszt, who was so impressed with him that he found him work in a piano shop and even let him share his home. In 1856 Raff moved to Wiesbaden, where he married, settled, and concentrated on composing and teaching music.

Swiss Composers

It was not until the 19th century that Swiss composers such as Joachim Raff achieved recognition. The German-Swiss composers Hermann Suter and Hans Huber gave their music a distinctive Swiss feel, with a blend of lyricism and piety, while the French-Swiss pair of Gustave Doret and Jacques-Dalcroze *(right)* brought an imaginative approach to orchestration. In this century, Swiss music that is free of French and German influences can be heard in the instrumental works of Ernst Bloch, Arthur Honegger, and Frank Martin, the operas of Heinrich Sutermeister, and the avant-garde music of oboist and composer Heinz Holliger.

EVENING RHAPSODY

THE NEW GERMAN SCHOOL

Most of Raff's early music reflected the strong influences of Mendelssohn and Schumann and was all written for piano. But during his days working for Liszt in the German city of Weimar *(right)*, Raff began to associate with a group of composers known as the *New German School*. Sharing in the school's high ideals for the future of German music, Raff made it his mission to combine the best of Switzerland's past and present musical traditions. Unfortunately, his efforts to reconcile different styles met with varying degrees of success.

LEADING COMPOSER

Raff was a prolific composer. He produced well over two hundred published works, including eleven symphonies, five concertos, music for the stage, chamber music, and a wealth of piano music. He was considered one of the leading composers of his day—ranking up with Brahms and Wagner. However, apart from *Evening Rhapsody*, his *Cavatina (right)*—a short melodic piece for violin and piano—is one of his few pieces that is remembered today.

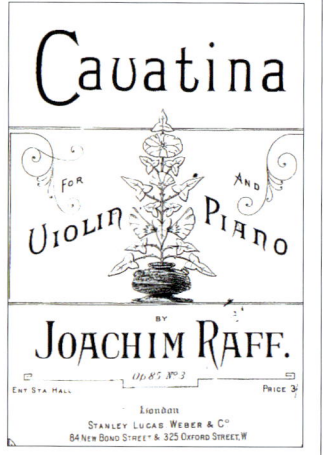

KEY NOTES

Raff was so confident that his compositions would survive the test of time that, according to his daughter Helene, he failed to make any provisions in his will for his family. As a result, all his unpublished material, including contributions from Helene, became the property of the Swiss state upon his death in 1882.

Cello Concerto: First Movement (Excerpt)

Sir Edward Elgar 1857–1934

Cello Concerto

First Movement (Excerpt)

Nowhere is Sir Edward Elgar's skill at writing for strings better demonstrated than in this haunting concerto. At its heart is a dialogue between a dreamy, reflective solo cello and a more emphatic orchestra. While the main melody on the strings is gently melancholy, the cello's part is full of brooding and despair—evoking the composer's native Worcestershire, as well as the change from the happy, carefree days of summer into the darker expanses of winter.

Elgar's Late Work

Elgar's *Cello Concerto*, completed in 1919, was his last significant orchestral work. Only transcriptions of other composers' works, a few occasional pieces, and a couple of suites were finished during the remaining fifteen years of his life, even though he was working on an opera and a third symphony when he died.

Key Notes

Elgar was quick to see the potential of the gramophone and he made many recordings of his music during the last twenty years of his life. The most famous was the recording of his Violin Concerto in 1932, featuring the sixteen-year-old Yehudi Menuhin.

A LONDON SYMPHONY: SECOND MOVEMENT

RALPH VAUGHAN WILLIAMS
1872–1958

A London Symphony

SECOND MOVEMENT

An atmosphere of intimate and reflective longing is conjured up by Vaughan Williams in the writing for the string instruments which opens this piece. The chords seem to hang in the air like the mists of a cold, foggy November day in London. A brooding cor anglais recalls Claude Debussy's *La Mer* ("The Sea"), after which a graceful viola introduces the middle section—a shimmering mass of sound punctuated by a stirring rhythm on sleigh bells. Each solo instrument adds its unique coloring to London life, as in the clarinet's imitation of a lavender-seller's street cry. A return of the opening brooding mood, with the French horn's distant calls, brings the movement to its mysterious end.

BLOOMSBURY CONNECTION

This movement is sometimes called *Bloomsbury Square on a November Afternoon*. This pre-World War I scene of Bloomsbury that Vaughan Williams depicts reflects his attachment to the area.

A London Symphony: Second Movement

Visionary and Nationalist

Vaughan Williams *(below)* was a man of the people in thought and action, a visionary and idealist who was always ready to devote himself to a cause. Even though he was forty-two years old, he enlisted in the army during World War I and served as an ambulance driver. After the war, he became director of music for the British Expeditionary Force, organizing music to be played by the troops. His music often reflected the aspirations of ordinary people. Vaughan Williams detested the Nazi regime of the 1930s and his campaigning on behalf of the German refugees led to the Nazi Party banning all his music. His strong nationalist sympathies are reflected in two of his essays, *Who Wants the English Composer?* and *National Music*.

Honors and Awards

Vaughan Williams refused to accept awards unless they honored his musical achievements. He said this was because he did not want to feel obliged to anyone in authority. As a result, he turned down many awards and appointments, including the offer of a knighthood. Those that he did accept include the Order of Merit in 1935, an honorary Doctorate of Music at Oxford, at least five other university doctorates, the prestigious Collard Life Fellowship, and, in 1955, the Albert Medal of the Royal Society of Arts *(above)*.

KEY NOTES

Vaughan Williams first conceived A London Symphony as a symphonic poem, before the composer George Butterworth advised him to turn it into a symphony. Vaughan Williams claimed it was not "programmatic" but "self-expressive," concluding that it must stand or fall as pure music.

IMAGES (FOR ORCHESTRA): GIGUES

CLAUDE DEBUSSY *1862–1918*

Images

(FOR ORCHESTRA): GIGUES

This piece is unmistakably impressionist in tone and is in the style most associated with Debussy. Inspired by the traditional song *The Keel Row*, which Debussy quotes in this third movement, the piece is rich in the variety of instrumentation. First the violin introduces the main theme, and then, one by one, other solo instruments rise out of a background of undulating string accompaniment. The tension continues to build as the woodwind section comes in and the percussion crackles as if there was an autumn storm in the air. The final, broad string melody bursts out with rolling kettledrums as the thunder arrives. Then, as the storm passes, the music dies away with a two-note call on the French horn.

THE THREE SETS OF IMAGES

Debussy wrote three sets of *Images*. The first two sets, in 1905 and 1907, were for solo piano. In 1905 he also began work on a set of three pieces for orchestra: "Gigues," "Ibéria," and "Rondes de Printemps." These three orchestral pieces were performed together for the first time in Paris in 1913.

IMAGES (FOR ORCHESTRA): GIGUES

THE WOMEN IN HIS LIFE

Debussy began work on his *Orchestral Images* the same year that his daughter Chou-Chou was born (1905) to him and his wife Emma Bardac *(right)*. The happy event was in marked contrast to the composer's history of stormy relationships with women. In 1889, while still a teenager, Debussy had begun a nine-year affair with Gabrielle Dupont. The partnership was punctuated with scandals, including a period when Debussy became engaged to the singer Thérèse Roger, as well as a suicide attempt by Gabrielle. Debussy married Lily Texier in 1899, but left her for Emma after five years. As a result, Lily attempted suicide. However, it seems the arrival of Chou-Chou had a settling effect on Debussy. He and Emma married in 1908 and stayed together for the remaining ten years of his life.

THE KEEL ROW

The origin of *The Keel Row*, the song that inspired "Gigues," is not clear. What is known is that it made its first appearance in print in *A Collection of Favourite Scots Tunes* around 1770. The tune closely resembles a number of English country dances, although it is now mainly associated with the fishing ports around the Newcastle and Tyneside district of northeastern England.

Right: *A fisherman's wife waits for his boat to return.*

KEY NOTES

The title "Gigues" is taken from the rustic dance or "jig" that originated in the late-16th century in Ireland, Scotland, and northern England. The dance, which rapidly spread to other parts of Europe, is a fast-paced and lively dance.

LIEUTENANT KIJÉ: ROMANCE

SERGEI PROKOFIEV *1891–1953*

Lieutenant Kijé

ROMANCE

Lieutenant Kijé was originally written as music for the 1933 film of the same name and remains one of Sergei Prokofiev's most popular compositions. The caustic humor of this symphonic suite does justice to the satirical mood of the original story. "Romance" conjures up a sentimental autumn scene with Kijé in love. Prokofiev shows an acute awareness of the orchestra's expressive potential from the opening solo double-bass in its top register (its most awkward area) to the bell-like sound of the celesta and the intentionally gushing strings—all combining perfectly to portray the hero of the piece.

THE STORY OF LIEUTENANT KIJÉ

Lieutenant Kijé tells of the comic career of a non-existent 19th-century Russian soldier who was created by a clerical error. To satisfy the eccentric Tsar Paul I's curiosity about this soldier, frightened officials are forced to exile the non-existent Kijé to Siberia, marry him off, promote him, and then abruptly kill him off as a hero.

LIEUTENANT KIJÉ: ROMANCE

COMPOSER IN EXILE

Taught by his mother, Sergei Prokofiev *(below)* had already composed his first opera by the age of nine. Joining the St. Petersburg Conservatory in 1904, he gained a reputation as an unruly student but still wrote his first major work, *Piano Concerto No.1*, and won the prestigious Rubinstein Prize. The turmoil surrounding the November 1917 Revolution, however, led him to question whether there was any place for his music in the new Russia. He left for America before settling in Paris. The period of exile proved to be a highly creative period during which he produced some of his most notable works. But he still yearned for his homeland and in 1933 he decided to return to Russia. Though he continued to compose, his later years were dogged by ill health and disagreements with the State. Prokofiev died of a brain hemorrhage in Moscow on March 5th, 1953—upstaged by Stalin, who died on the same day.

STALIN'S DECREE

After the Union of Soviet Composers was set up by Josef Stalin *(right)* in 1932, Russian music fell under political control. In 1948 the Communist Party condemned several leading Russian composers, notably Prokofiev and Shostakovich, for writing music "marked with formalist perversions...alien to the Soviet people" and banned a large number of their earlier works. A firm believer in "music for the people," Prokofiev attempted a compromise but failed to satisfy the authorities. Many of his works were not performed in Russia until the 1960s. Shostakovich, winner of the Stalin Prize in 1940 and "composer-laureate of the Soviet State," found it even more difficult to gain official acceptance but still continued to compose prolifically.

LIEUTENANT KIJÉ: ROMANCE

THE PARIS YEARS

Prokofiev found the time spent in France from the spring of 1920 to 1933 to be highly inspirational. He had already met the impresario Diaghilev, in London in 1914, and their renewed friendship in Paris led to commissions for the Ballets Russes, including the *The Steel Step* and *The Prodigal Son (right)*. Paris presented a real challenge for Prokofiev; the people seemed impossible to shock—they had heard it all before—and works that offended the critics elsewhere were well received here. Twice, in 1923 and 1924, requests came from Leningrad for Prokofiev to return and he visited in 1927. He was, however, unwilling to forego the musical and intellectual climate of the French capital, and it was not until 1933 that he finally returned.

AN UNEASY FRIENDSHIP

Much of the reputed rivalry between Stravinsky *(right)* and Prokofiev seems to have been stirred up by the press. For instance, in his autobiography, Stravinsky referred to Prokofiev as "this remarkable musician." And, there is little doubt that Stravinsky was a major influence on Prokofiev, especially in his *Rite of Spring*, even though he refused to acknowledge Stravinsky's influence in public.

KEY NOTES

As well as Lieutenant Kijé, Prokofiev wrote the music for other films, including several for the legendary director Sergei Eisenstein. The film score of Lieutenant Kijé was never actually published, though Prokofiev later arranged it into a symphonic suite, "Romance" being one of its five movements.

The Seasons: Autumn ("Bacchanale" and "Petit Adagio")

Alexander Glazunov 1865–1936

The Seasons

Autumn ("Bacchanale" and "Petit Adagio")

The Seasons is a one-act ballet made up of four linked scenes corresponding to each of the four seasons. Autumn is the fourth and final section and is by far the most boisterous of Glazunov's seasonal interpretations. The jolly "Bacchanale," opens with a wild, Slavonic theme on the strings. With more than a hint of Tchaikovsky at his passionate best, the scope is cinematic, conjuring up the vast expanses of the Russian countryside as the workers gather in the autumn harvest. The less vigorous "Petit Adagio" introduces a lighter feel to the work, a well-earned break of merriment for the harvesters, before the main theme returns.

One-Act Ballet

The Seasons was first staged in 1900 at St. Petersburg. The cast featured the best of Russian ballet, including the first-created role for the nineteen-year-old Anna Pavlova. The "Bacchanale" from *Autumn*, in particular, became closely associated with the great ballerina and her personal repertory.

The Seasons: Autumn ("Bacchanale" and "Petit Adagio")

A Life at the Conservatory

Born in St. Petersburg in 1865, Glazunov *(right)* had completed a successful First Symphony by the age of sixteen. After studying under Rimsky-Korsakov, Glazunov became increasingly involved in St. Petersburg's

musical life and was appointed a professor at the city's conservatory in 1899. Six years later, and now an international figure, he was appointed director of the conservatory—a post he held for the next twenty-five years. In this role he worked tirelessly and in 1922 was named "The People's Artist of the Republic." The burdens of administrative work gradually wore him down, however, affecting his creativity and health, and toward the end of his directorship, he had to take extended leave abroad. He settled in Paris in 1932, dying there four years later.

Teacher and Friend

When Rimsky-Korsakov became fourteen-year-old Glazunov's private teacher, a lifelong friendship was made. Under the elder man's guidance, Glazunov learned much, particularly from his dynamic orchestration. They even worked together to complete Alexander Borodin's unfinished material. Glazunov was said to have written down the overture for the opera *Prince Igor* simply by remembering how Borodin had once played it. Glazunov was always loyal to Rimsky-Korsakov, even resigning from the conservatory after his friend was dismissed for sympathizing with the students who were striking. Glazunov returned eight months later to fill the post vacated by his mentor.

The Seasons: Autumn ("Bacchanale" and "Petit Adagio")

The Belyayev Circle

Recognizing Alexander Glazunov's talents, the Russian art patron and music publisher Mitrofan Belyayev introduced him to his composer friends, known as the Belyayev Circle *(below)*, who used to meet in St. Petersburg during the 1880s. Glazunov was soon drawn to them, including Rimsky-Korsakov, Borodin, and Scriabin. In many ways, the circle was a natural progression of the "Five" (the 19th-century group of Russian composers that included Rimsky-Korsakov and Borodin) in that most of its members were nationalists. But the new group did not see itself as revolutionary so much as progressive. Belyayev devoted much of his time and wealth to promoting members of his circle, especially Glazunov, whom he helped financially.

Eminent Visitors

Even eminent figures such as Glazunov were affected by the deprivations that befell Russia in the aftermath of the Civil War in the 1920s. Times were hard and Glazunov found himself sharing two rooms with his elderly mother. His popularity and genial nature, however, meant that his small flat soon became a regular stopover for many eminent musicians and writers. The German conductors Otto Klemperer and Hermann Abendroth, the Austrian pianist Artur Schnabel, and even the English novelist H.G. Wells *(right)* were all frequent guests.

Key Notes

Though regarded as old-fashioned by some of his successors, Glazunov was one of the first composers to write music specifically for the saxophone, producing a saxophone quartet in 1932 and a saxophone concerto in 1934.

Credits & Acknowledgments

PICTURE CREDITS

Cover /Title and Contents Pages/ IBC: Images Colour Library/AKG London: 7(tl), 14(t); Bridgeman Art Library, London/Johnny Van Haeften Gallery, London (Issak Ouwater: A view in Amsterdam): 3; National Museam of American Art, Washington (Childe Hassam:Improvisation): 4; Private Collection (E.W. White:The Fall of the Leaf): 5; Victoria & Albert Museam, London (Frederick Walker: Autumn): 9; Chrisitie's, London (Emanuel Labhardt:View of the Lake of Zurich):13(tr); Christies, London (J.A. Grimshaw:In the Golden Glow of Autumn): (16); National Gallery of Scotland (Gustave Courbet:The wave): 18; British Library, London: 14 (b); Eye Ubiquitous: 10, 15; Mary Evans Picture Library: 6(tr), 11(t & b), 13(tl), 19(r), 25(b), 21(r); Fine Art Photographic Library/Baumkotter Gallery (Sebastien Vrancx:The Harvest): 2; Anthony Mitchell Fine Paintings (G.Hodgson: A Garden at Warwick): 8; (H.Hadfield Cudley:An Alpine Landscape):12; (Frederick Vigers: Lover's Lane): 20; Lebrecht Collection: 6(tl & b), 7(tr & bl & cr), 11(c), 13(br), 17(l), 19(l), 21(l), 22(t & b), 24(t & b), 25(t); Performing Arts Library/Emma Gregg: 3(l); RSA: Albert medal: 17(r); Sotheby's Picture Library/ (A.von Wierusz-Kowalski; Peasant Girls Riding on a Haycart): 23.

All illustrations and symbols: John See